Learn
English Paper Piecing
by MACHINE™

Designs by Julie Higgins

HOUSE of
WHITE
BIRCHES

PUBLISHERS
SINCE 1947

Learn English Paper Piecing by Machine

When my career entailed working with finance and investments, I spent free lunch times not only at the local fabric shop stroking fabrics, but also at a wonderful antique mall. It was dark and cool in this three-story building, and it was stuffed with beautiful items of the past. I especially liked to browse through the antique quilts on display.

I walked in one day, looked up and saw a beautiful Grandmother's Flower Garden quilt

hanging over a balcony. It just struck me—I loved the quilt. Until that moment, I hadn't even known I liked that type of quilt.

That night, I told my husband Roger about the quilt. He said, "Buy it if you like it." I said, "No. If I want one, I can make one." I had never tried English paper piecing, but I figured it was time to learn.

I purchased a package of the little paper hexagons that are sold for use in this method. According to the instructions, you baste all the fabric edges over the paper with a needle and thread, and then sew them together by hand. I don't enjoy handwork. I love hearing the hum of my sewing machine and relish the speed at which I can bring my ideas to completion. Though I suspected the English paper-piecing method wouldn't work for me, I was willing to give it a go, but did decide to use a glue stick for the basting process.

Joking that it might take me 30 years to get it done, I cut and glued, cut and glued. Then I started whipstitching the pieces together. It didn't take long for my fingers to get sore. My stitches didn't look all that good either. It was tedious, boring and slow. Worst of all, it took four–six hours to sew one block. I thought I might need more than 30 years.

I began hauling baggies with me everywhere I went, thinking that there had to be a better way. I'm sure my husband got tired of hearing the

It was so easy to sew these little pieces together by machine that I assumed someone must have done it before, and I didn't know about it. I asked other quilters. I read. I searched the Internet. I couldn't find any reference to English paper piecing by machine. That's when I really started to experiment and play.

This book is a result of that play and the desire on my part to save other machine lovers the misery of sore fingers and tedium.

Since that day, I've developed a personal theory. I've picked up unfinished Grandmother's Flower Garden blocks at antique malls, flea markets, yard sales, etc. If you notice, you'll only find four–eight of them at a time. My theory is that the person who started them never lived long enough to finish the whole quilt.

increasing level of whining and griping because one evening he said, "Well, why don't you just sew it on your machine?" Well, you're not supposed to sew it on a machine. It's always been done by hand. But, after I sat there for a moment, I finally replied, "You know, I've been thinking about a way I might be able to sew the hexagons together by machine, but I don't know if it would work or not." "Well, quit griping and try it. What have you got to lose?"

In our 27 years of marriage the war cry "What have we got to lose?" has gotten us into all kinds of situations. So, that statement was all it took. I tried my idea and it worked! I couldn't believe how incredibly easy it was. I sewed another block. What had taken me four–six hours to sew by hand was finished in 15 minutes by machine— unbelievable! Roger timed me with his watch for three more blocks. Each block took 15 minutes. I looked at the stitches. They looked better than the one I stitched with a needle, and I was sure they were much more secure. I was amazed.

I'm here to tell you that you too can finish a Grandmother's Flower Garden quilt in your lifetime. If you really do like to piece by hand, you will still be able to use the patterns in this book. You don't have to sew them by machine just because I do.

One more thing I would like to point out before we get down to business is that this is only a starting point. I haven't been using this technique for 20 years, so I know there is room for improvement. There are so many smart, creative and ingenious quilters out there. I hope you will take this infant idea and expand, develop and improve it. Find a shortcut I've missed. Share your discovery with others and with me. Most importantly, just have fun. ■

Meet the Designer
Julie Higgins

Julie Higgins started sewing when she was 12 years old, but, didn't begin making quilts until 2000. She has been enthusiastically learning, teaching, speaking to quilters and designing ever since.

Her quilt Owinja won a Judge's Choice Award in the 2003 Miniatures from the Heart Contest, and her quilts have been juried into the 2003 Hoffman and 2003 Sulky Loves America exhibits. She has also won awards at regional shows and fairs. Many of her designs have been published in McCalls *Quick Quilts*.

Her best advice to other quilters is to keep an open mind and try everything. Hook up with other people who love what you love, be it at a quilting guild, a quilting bee or an Internet group. You just can't find a better group of people.

In Julie's "other life" she is a certified financial planner who spent 23 years working in investment-related fields. She and her husband own a party-tent rental business in Bloomington, Ind., and she left investments to work with her husband, daughter and son full-time. Her office assistant is little and fuzzy, and he takes frequent naps at her feet.

Dedication

I welcome this opportunity to thank my husband, Roger, and my daughter, Becky, for giving me their love, support and tolerance in my quilting endeavors (especially the tolerance part!).

I wish to thank my friends in the Bloomington (Indiana) Quilters's Guild. Your oohs and aahs and words of encouragement have meant more to me than words can express.

I also want to thank the staff at House of White Birches for their hard work. In particular, I appreciate the help from my editor, Jeanne

Stauffer, and her assistant, Dianne Schmidt, for their expertise and for giving me the opportunity to share my work.

Thank you, Debbie Bortniak, for giving my instructions a try. Thank you, Jane Pitt, for quilting Purple Haze so beautifully.

Last, I want to thank the quilters who have decided to try something new and have purchased this book. I really hope you enjoy this technique as much as I have.

Table of Contents

General Instructions

Traditional English Paper Piecing vs. English Paper Piecing by Machine

If you are interested in traditional English paper piecing, there are many techniques and pattern books available. Paper templates usually come with instructions right in the package.

Traditionally, paper piecing is accomplished by using some type of template made from card stock or paper. There are also reusable plastic templates that pop out of the finished piece. You must cut your fabric a little larger than the template so that you can hand-baste the fabric around the template. When using paper, you may baste right through the paper. Then, placing the pieces right sides together, you whipstitch the pieces together with thread and needle, remove the basting thread, and then remove the template. If you need more advice about how to use hand-stitching methods, I am not the person to ask.

Let's compare the differences between the hand and machine methods of English paper piecing.

HAND VS. MACHINE

Making Templates
For Hand Method: Create paper templates (buying templates for either method would be the same).

For Machine Method: Create freezer-paper templates—you can cut more than one at a time accurately.

Cutting Fabric
For Hand Method: Draw around each template and add approximately ¼" allowance when cutting out.

For Machine Method: Line up rows of freezer-paper templates on the wrong side of the fabric. Eyeball ½" in between templates and give a quick press to the template. Cut out several rows at a time. Templates do not slip on fabric.

Basting Fabric to Template
For Hand Method: Using needle and thread, fold fabric around each edge of template and baste in place.

For Machine Method: Rub a washable glue stick around the edge of the template and seam allowance. Fold seam allowance over the template to glue-baste in place.

Sewing
For Hand Method: Using needle and thread, whipstitch each of the pieces together. If you are really good, your stitches should not show. This is a portable project (which is good because you will have to spend every spare minute you have working on it).

For Machine Method: Use your sewing machine and a small zigzag stitch to whipstitch your pieces together. You will see the stitches if using cotton thread. If this bothers you, use invisible thread for the stitching.

Finishing

For Hand Method: Remove basting thread and remove paper.

For Machine Method: By using glue, you must place a damp towel on the blocks for about 10 minutes in order to remove the papers. Just remember, you don't have to watch the towel, so go sew another block.

FABRIC SELECTION

I recommend using 100 percent cotton fabrics. Prewashing is a personal choice. I don't unless I think the colors will bleed. You will be wetting the fabrics to remove the freezer paper when you finish the blocks, so if they are going to bleed, they will do so then.

Your design will dictate the color of the fabrics you use. As you will see, some designs will use high-contrast fabrics while in others you will want the pieces to blend so there will be less contrast. The fun thing about using your template is that you can fussy-cut by placing the template exactly over a motif you want to use, and what you cover is what you get as shown by the bug in the center of one motif in Photo 1.

Photo 1

WHAT YOU NEED

• Sewing Machine: You must have a sewing machine capable of sewing a zigzag stitch. I have found that a smaller sharp needle (No. 70 or under) works well.

• Thread: Size 50 thread in a color to match fabrics is the best choice. However, a neutral color thread will work if you don't have thread to match each fabric. You may also use a clear monofilament thread, but you must use it in the bobbin as well as in the top of the machine if you want the stitches to be totally invisible.

• Freezer paper: This is usually sold by the roll at most grocery stores. One side is plastic coated.

• Glue stick: It doesn't matter what kind as long as it says washable and acid-free. The least expensive kind can be found with office and school supplies. Make sure to buy the clear glue, not the purple-color sticks.

• Old cutting mat: I like to use my cutting mat as a gluing surface. Any excess glue comes off easily with water, and your piece does not stick to the mat like it would if you used paper to protect your surface. I can set the mat on my lap and watch television while I'm glue basting.

• Rotary cutter

• Rotary-cutting ruler: to cut strips

• Square ruler: This comes in handy for squaring up quilts and pillows.

• Paper scissors

• Fabric scissors

• Appliqué scissors

• Heavy template plastic

• Retractable lead pencil

• Iron and ironing surface

• Fabric

PREPARE PAPER TEMPLATES

Although you can buy paper templates that will work even with glue basting, the price does add up if you make many quilts.

Patterns are given at the end of these instructions for the template sizes needed to complete all the projects in this book. Use the patterns to make your own paper templates. It is less expensive though it obviously takes more time than buying precut templates. However, I like the less stiff feel of freezer paper, and adhering the freezer paper to the fabric makes it easier to cut out the shapes; the freezer paper doesn't move on the fabric.

Trace the templates provided in this book onto heavy template plastic and cut them out on the drawn line. You will need only one plastic template for each shape you want to use.

Tear off three or four same-size sheets of freezer paper. Layer them one on top of the other, making sure all the sheets are facing the same way (plastic side down). Lay them on your ironing board, shiny side down and paper side up. With your iron set at perma-press (no steam), lightly press the layers just until they stick together (usually a second or two). You only want them to stick together long enough to trace on them and cut them apart. Take the stack to your worktable.

Place the plastic template on the top of your stack (paper side up). Using a retractable lead pencil, trace around the template, making sure to keep your lead as close as possible to the template for accuracy and consistency. Don't leave much room between the tracings because you will be cutting them out on the drawn line. Using paper scissors, cut out each shape. Gently fluff the shape to loosen the pressed pieces. You will have three or four freezer-paper pieces from each one you trace and cut out.

If you find you like paper piecing, you may want to invest in a die cutter. This consists of a die (a sharp piece of metal embedded in spongy rubber) and a machine that you roll the die through. You can layer eight to 10 sheets of freezer paper and easily cut multiples of the same shape at once. Because I use so many templates, I invested in a GrandeMark Roller Die Cutting System made by Accu-Cut. I can use this machine to cut multiple layers of paper or fabric. One of my favorite dies has six 1" hexagons on it, and by layering 10 pieces of freezer paper, I can cut 60 templates each time I roll the die through the machine. Accu-Cut has a new, smaller system that will also accommodate this die called the Zip'eMate Personal Die Cutting Machine.

PREPARE THE FABRIC PIECES

Place the fabric wrong side up on your ironing surface. Set your iron on a cotton setting or slightly lower, with no steam. Press to remove wrinkles. Line up the freezer-paper templates on the wrong side of the fabric, placing them with as little waste between as possible. Leave about ½" of fabric showing between all the edges of the paper templates as shown in Photo 2.

Photo 2

Press as you go. I usually lay down five or six paper pieces, set the warm iron on them until they stick, lay down 5 or 6 more and repeat the process.

Cut around each template, leaving an approximate ¼" seam allowance as shown in Photo 3.

Photo 3

Run the glue stick around the edge of the fabric on the paper side of the template unit. You can rub glue on some of the edge of the freezer paper as well; it will just help to hold it better.

Carefully fold each edge of the fabric up and over the edge of the template to glue-baste in place (Photo 4). Add an additional little swipe of glue as you fold each hexagonal corner to hold the fold.

Hint
I do my glue work on an old cutting mat. You can also use a lap tray and watch television while you glue. After I have glued and folded the edges, I turn the finished unit right side up and push it down securely on the mat, running my finger around the edge, so I get crisp folded edges. Let them dry for just a few minutes.

You can tell where the edge of the freezer paper is, so make sure you don't fold the paper. If you do, your shape will not end up being a hexagon.

Photo 4

FUSSY CUTTING
Fussing cutting is an easy technique that can result in fun and surprises. Fussy cutting just means that rather than cutting your fabric as it falls, whether by rotary cutter or template, you instead pick a particular area to cut out.

Photo 5

Photo 5 shows a vintage diamond-shape hexagon quilt block in which the quilter had fussy-cut the

Photo 6

flowers. You can see that each petal has the exact same bloom. This quilter purposefully placed her template over one of the flowers in a piece of fabric and cut it out. She then moved the template from place to place in the fabric in order to cut out the same exact flower 11 more times. When you get done, the fabric resembles Swiss cheese as shown in Figure 1.

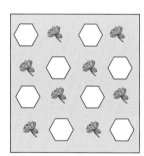

Figure 1

You may want to use a printed motif that is larger than your template. This can be accomplished. Make sure you have enough of the same exact motifs in your fabric, and you can piece them together.

For example, one of the fish hiding under the 3-D petal in Froggy's Flower Garden (Photo 6) is too big to fit on one template. My hexagons were ½" and the fish was about ⅞" long. I needed to use two of the same fish motifs and two hexagon templates in order to create one whole fish.

To accomplish this, first, line up the freezer-paper template on half of one printed motif as shown in Figure 2. Cut out as usual, with an approximate ¼" seam allowance. Glue-baste the edges.

Figure 2

For the second half of the fish, line up a second freezer-paper template with the edge exactly aligned on an identical fish shape in the same place that the edge of the first freezer-paper template left off as shown in Figure 3.

Figure 3

When you turn the seam allowances under for the second template and place the two templates side by side, the two fish parts match up, creating one continuous fish as shown in Figure 4.

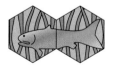

Figure 4

MACHINE-APPLIQUÉ OPTIONS

The blocks in this book are constructed by paper piecing a shape from hexagons or diamonds and appliquéing the finished shape to a background.

Traditional appliqué shapes are required in some projects such as the leaves in Grape Harvest and Simply Orchids. Many books are available about the many techniques of appliqué if you need in-depth instruction. I will provide only a brief overview of machine-appliqué techniques that can be used to create the projects in this book.

Prepare the Appliqué

If you are making a shape such as a hexagonal flower or a diamond star, your piece is ready to appliqué as soon as the paper piecing is done. The edges are all ready because they have been glue-basted. All you need to do is press the piece flat.

For other shapes, such as leaves, you may appliqué them by machine in a couple of different ways.

Using Freezer Paper

Trace the templates onto the paper side of freezer paper and cut out on the drawn line. Press the freezer-paper template to the wrong side of the fabric. Cut around the template leaving approximately ¼" seam allowance. Using a glue stick, glue-baste the edges over the template. Trim points and clip curves as you baste in order to get a nice smooth edge.

Using Fusible Web

If you don't want a turned-under edge, you may use fusible web. Trace the templates directly onto the paper side of the fusible web. Cut out the templates, leaving approximately ¼" around the outside edge. Place the paper shape on the wrong side of the fabric; press following the manufacturer's instructions. Cut out the shape on the drawn line; remove paper backing and fuse

to the background. **Note:** *If your shape is large, you may remove the center of the fusible paper shape before ironing it to the fabric to reduce bulk, leaving only the outside edges to fuse to the background.*

Preparing the Background

When planning machine appliqué, it is always wise to oversize the background blocks by ¼"–½". The background block may get distorted depending on your fabric, method of appliqué or machine stitch, especially if using a machine satin or zigzag stitch. The use of a fabric stabilizer helps to reduce distortions and keep fabric from puckering during stitching. There are several types of fabric stabilizer, including tear-off and water-soluble versions. Refer to the instructions included with the product for use.

Registration marks on the background help with positioning of pieces. The easiest way to do this is to fold the background block vertically, horizontally and diagonally and finger-press folds. When the block is opened, there should be light creases in the fabric that may be used as placement guides.

Sewing Appliqué Shapes to the Background

Once the appliqué shapes are placed on the background, either pin or use small dabs of glue stick to glue-baste in place. Using a small zigzag stitch, machine blanket-stitch or your favorite stitch, sew around the shape. If you don't want the stitches to show, use invisible thread. Or use a fancy stitch with a specialty thread if you want to make a statement and you are confident of your stitch quality.

Finishing the Appliqué
Trimming Appliqué

When machine-appliquéing without the use of fusible web, the background layer may be trimmed away to reduce bulk. After stitching

Photo 7

Photo 8

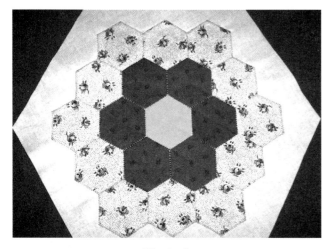

Photo 9

shapes to the background, turn it over. From the back of the block, you will see the stitching line. Using appliqué scissors, if you have them, or regular scissors, carefully cut away the background ¼" inside the stitching line under the appliqué shapes to reveal the paper templates (Photo 7). *Note: If you used fusible web for appliqué, you will not be able to trim away the background layers.*

Remove Paper Templates

Place the block on a waterproof surface such as the old mat used for gluing.

Wet a terrycloth hand towel and wring it out. Lay a damp towel on the back of the block for about 10 minutes to moisten the glue to allow easy removal of the freezer-paper templates (Photo 8). Give the block another pressing to finish (Photo 9).

HEXAGONAL CONSTRUCTION TECHNIQUE

When constructing a Grandmother's Flower Garden block, begin sewing from the center and move in an outward circular motion, adding petals as you progress. You may continuously sew all six petals to the center hexagon without lifting the needle or cutting the thread by just raising the presser foot at the end of a sewing line.

1. Set the sewing machine: Select the narrowest zigzag stitch that you can control. You need to catch the edge of the hexagons you are sewing. You don't want the stitches to be far apart, but you don't want a close satin stitch either. Set the machine to mimic the size stitch you would use if you were sewing by hand. Photo 10 shows a good size.

Photo 10

2. Place the center hexagon and one "petal" hexagon right sides together with the center hexagon on the bottom and the petal lying face down on top of the center as shown in Photo 11, aligning the edges to be stitched.

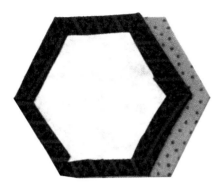

Photo 11

Photo 12

3. Start stitching with the needle in the down position if you have that feature on the sewing machine. Be sure the needle is positioned to the right-hand side of the zigzag, ready to come up and take the bite to the left. *Note: Test the stitch on a scrap first. Stop the needle in the correct*

position, remove the scrap and replace with the hexagon, put the needle down and begin to stitch.

4. Align one side of the two layered hexagons to the left next to the sewing-machine needle (actually touching the needle, which is in the down position). You will be sewing down the right-hand side of the hexagon. Referring to Photo 12, start stitching from the corner of the hexagon farthest away from you and work your way along the edge until you get to the front corner. Take one bite in the fabric, making sure your next stitch goes off the fabric. Zig into the fabric, then zag off the fabric. **Note:** *This is what I like to call a machine whipstitch.* End the stitching with the needle in the position to the right again, needle down. Do not cut the thread.

Hint

I personally don't like to take time to do a locking stitch, and with this block, you will be appliquéing the edges down later. But, when I feel like I need an extra stitch for durability, I manually hold onto my hexagon unit until the stitch is made, then let the feed dogs go ahead with their job. It's like a mini-tug-of-war, but you can easily hold it in place for that extra zigzag stitch and never have to reach for a lever or button.

5. Once you have completed this stitching line, raise the presser foot and swing the unit to the left in a counterclockwise movement. Carefully open the petal without pulling it away from the needle in the process. Give the petal a little pull away from the center hexagon to make it lie flat.

This also opens the machine whipstitch. Turn the unit back to the right slightly to align the next stitching line and get ready for the second petal as shown in Photo 13.

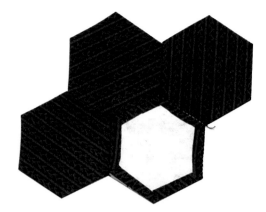

Photo 14

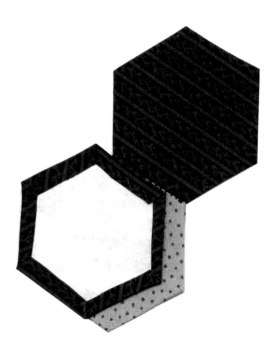

Photo 13

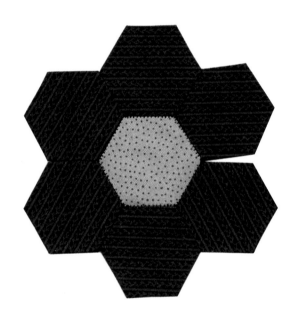

Photo 15

6. Layer the second petal face down on the center hexagon as in step 2. Push the far corner edge up against the needle, which has been left down and to the right in the zag position. Now you will zig into the fabric again as in step 4 along the second edge of the center hexagon. As you near the end of this stitching line, raise the presser foot, open up the petal and pull it to the right side; give it a little tug. Proceed in this manner until all six hexagon petals are attached to the center hexagon, referring to Photos 14 and 15. There will be one continuous seam around the outer edge of the center hexagon as the petals are attached.

7. Raise the presser foot again, fold the entire flower in half, lining up the edges of the inside of the two petals you will be sewing next. Sew the seam from the center of the flower to the outside edge.

Hint

Fold the pieces in half if you need to line them up as shown in Photo 16, just as you would if you were hand piecing. Freezer paper folds much easier than many of the paper units sold on the market. The most important thing to remember is to keep your edges even and to use a small stitch, but make sure to catch the edge of both hexagons. If you miss an edge of one of the hexagons (usually on the bottom), just put them back together with the missed edge on the top and resew. If it happens too frequently, set a little wider stitch width. Check your edges as you go.

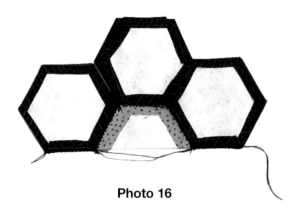

Photo 16

8. Continue sewing all of the inner seams of the flower, folding as necessary. ***Note:*** *You will be able to tell if the units are straight because the outside petals will align and the inner hexagon will always be folded exactly in half.* Pull out what thread you need to get to the next seam, sewing some from the inside out and some from the outside in without fastening off the thread. Trim all threads after the flower is complete. This is a good place to take that little extra stitch at the beginning and end of each line of stitching. This will complete one six-petaled flower; press flat with iron.

FINALLY

Learn to English Paper Piece by Machine speeds up the progress of your work tremendously. It is easy to sew a double flower in 15 minutes. Once you understand this technique, your next six-petaled flower will take you 5–10 minutes to sew.

It is easy to add petals. Work in a circular motion, folding and creasing where necessary and sewing as many seams together as possible without cutting the thread. It's much easier to take an extra stitch and move the flower an inch than it is to cut the thread each time.

When all stitching is complete, trim all threads on the back of each petal.

Flowers can have six, 18, 36 or more petals as shown in Photo 17.

Photo 17

This same technique may be used for other shapes such as diamonds. Several projects in this book use other shapes.

There is one caveat for this technique: the larger your piece becomes, the harder it is to fold and refold your work. You could make a quilt with all hexagons, but it will become bulky and hard to handle (also true if you are piecing by hand).

I prefer to piece my shapes and then appliqué them to a background or background block.

As you try this technique with your own designs, think about which pieces you would put together if you were sewing by hand and then look for shortcuts. This technique could be used as a speedy remedy for many existing designs. ■

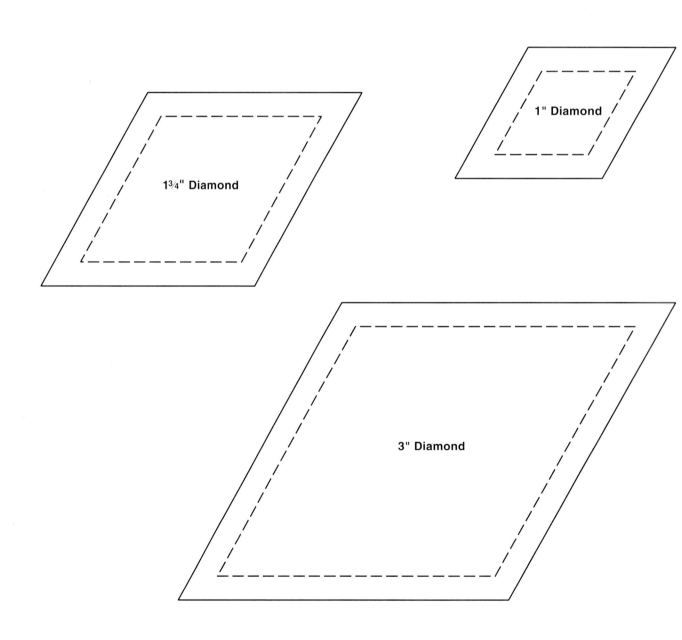

1" Diamond

1¾" Diamond

3" Diamond

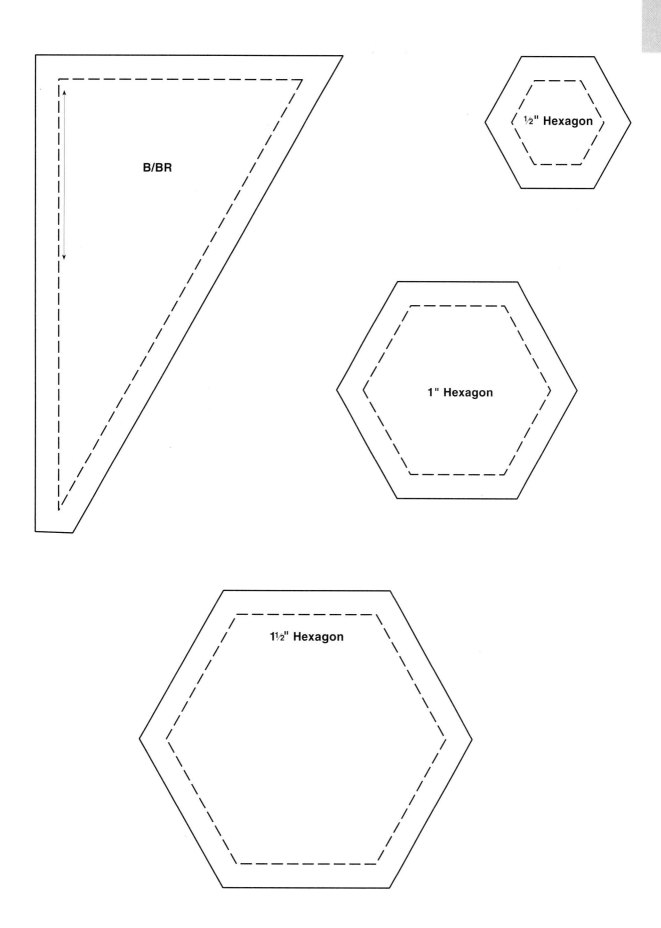

B/BR

½" Hexagon

1" Hexagon

1½" Hexagon

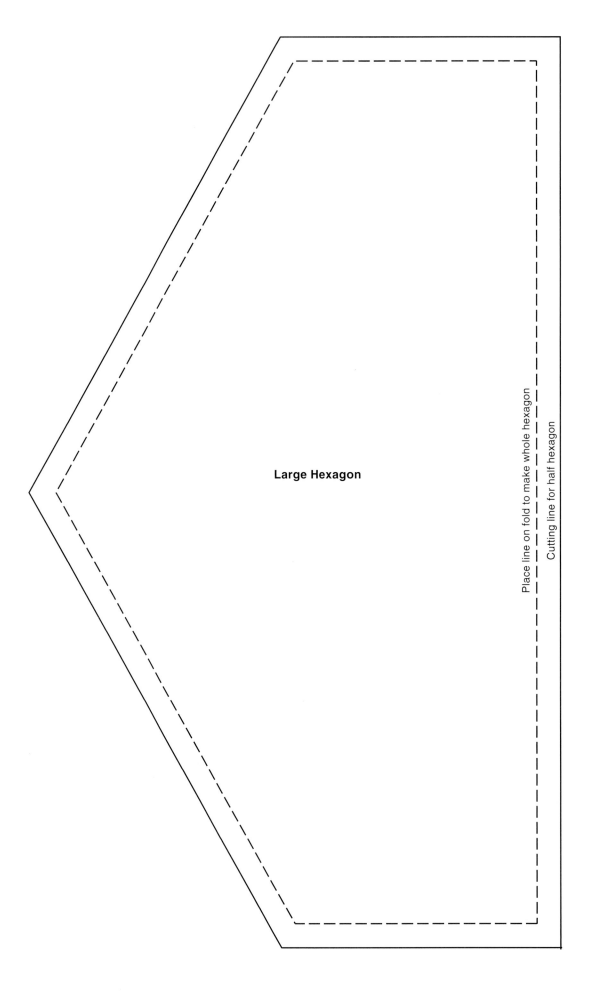

Large Hexagon

Place line on fold to make whole hexagon

Cutting line for half hexagon

Vintage Garden Quilt

Reproduction prints combine with vintage fabrics from my stash to make a quilt like Grandmother's.

PROJECT NOTES
Can you spot the real vintage fabrics in this pretty quilt? Try fussy-cutting motifs to create an I Spy quilt. The options are endless.

The background hexagon is sized to give the illusion of 1" hexagonal paths between each of the blossoms.

PROJECT SPECIFICATIONS
Skill Level: Intermediate
Quilt Size: 58½" x 68¾"
Block Size: 9" x 10⅜"
Number of Blocks: 28
Templates Used: 1" and Large hexagons

FABRIC & BATTING
- ¼ yard yellow solid
- 1 yard green solid
- 1 yard total scraps for inner flower petals
- 1½ yards total scraps for outer flower petals
- 1½ yards total scraps for outer border
- 4 yards white solid
- Backing 64" x 75"
- Batting 64" x 75"

SUPPLIES & TOOLS
- Thread to match fabrics
- Freezer paper
- Glue stick
- Basic sewing tools and supplies

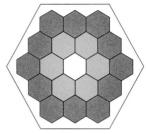

Vintage Garden
9" x 10⅜"

Cutting
1. Prepare template for A using Large Hexagon pattern given on page 18; cut 28 whole A and four half A hexagons white solid.

2. Prepare template for B using pattern given on page 17; cut two each B and BR white solid.

3. Prepare templates for C and G using patterns given; cut as directed on each piece. *pg 23*

4. To complete one flower, prepare one yellow center, six inner petals from one fabric and 12 outer petals from another fabric using the 1" hexagon pattern on page 17 and referring to the General Instructions. Repeat for 28 flowers (532 total 1" hexagons).

5. Cut three 5¼" by fabric width strips white solid. Join strips on short ends to make one long strip; subcut strip into two 54½" D strips.

6. Cut three 4¼" by fabric width strips white solid. Join strips on short ends to make one long strip; subcut strip into two 51¾" E strips.

7. Cut two 6⅜" by fabric width strips white solid; subcut strips into (11) 6⅜" squares. Cut each square in half on both diagonals to make 44 F triangles.

8. Cut 2½"-wide bias strips green solid to total 370" for binding.

Completing the Blocks

1. Join the 1" hexagon pieces for one flower beginning with the yellow center, adding six inner petals and 12 outer petals referring to the General Instructions. Repeat for 28 flowers.

2. Fold each A piece horizontally and vertically; crease to mark centers. Center one flower on each A hexagon, referring to Figure 1. Machine-stitch in place referring to the General Instructions.

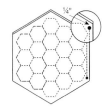

Figure 3

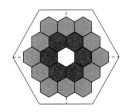

Figure 1

3. Cut away A from behind the appliquéd flowers and remove freezer-paper pieces referring to the General Instructions.

4. Repeats steps 2 and 3 to complete 28 blocks.

Completing the Top

1. Join six blocks to make a row referring to Figure 2; repeat for three six-block rows. Press seams open. **Note:** *When joining blocks, stop stitching at the end of the seam allowance (Figure 3), not at the end of the piece, to allow for easy seaming when joining rows.*

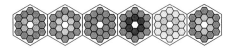

Figure 2

Vintage Garden Quilt
Placement Diagram
58½" x 68¾"

2. Join five blocks and two half A pieces to make a row as shown in Figure 4; repeat for two rows. Press seams open.

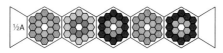

Figure 4

3. Join the rows, referring to the Placement Diagram for positioning; press seams open.

4. Set-in C pieces at sides and add B and BR pieces to the corners to complete the pieced center; press seams toward B and C pieces.

5. Sew a D strip to opposite long sides of the pieced center; press seams toward D strips.

6. Sew an E strip to the top and bottom of the pieced center; press seams toward E strips.

7. Join 12 F and 11 G pieces for a side border strip as shown in Figure 5; press seams toward G. Repeat for two side border strips. Sew a strip to opposite long sides of the pieced center; press seams toward D.

8. Join 10 F and nine G pieces for top border strip, again referring to Figure 5; press seams toward G. Repeat for bottom border strip. Sew a strip to the top and bottom of the pieced center; press seams toward E.

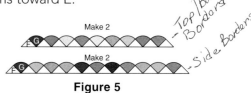

Figure 5

9. Join two G pieces; repeat for four G units. Press seams open. Sew a G unit to each corner to complete the quilt top.

Finishing the Quilt

1. Sandwich the batting between the prepared backing and the completed top; pin or baste layers to hold.

2. Quilt as desired by hand or machine; trim edges even and remove pins or basting. **Note**: *The quilt shown was machine-quilted in a stipple design in the white solid background areas around a marked design that appears as trapunto because of the stipple quilting.*

3. Join bias binding strips on short ends to make a long strip; press seams open. Press strip in half along length with wrong sides together.

4. Pin bias binding to the right side of the quilted top, aligning raw edges. Stitch all around, pulling inverted angles straight as you stitch, allowing the binding to pleat a little after stitching as shown in Figure 6. Overlap at beginning and end.

Figure 6

5. Turn the binding to the wrong side; hand- or machine-stitch in place to finish. ∎

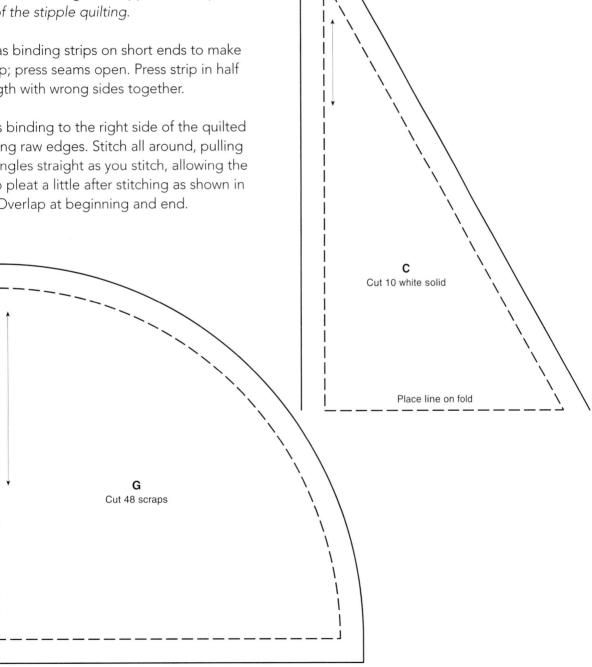

C
Cut 10 white solid

Place line on fold

G
Cut 48 scraps

Vintage Garden Pillow

One flower motif is highlighted with red piping in this pretty pillow.

Flower
Placement Diagram
9" x 10⅜"

PROJECT SPECIFICATIONS

Skill Level: Intermediate
Pillow Size: 14⅜" x 14½"
Block Size: 9" x 10⅜"
Number of Blocks: 1
Templates Used: 1" and Large hexagons

FABRIC & BATTING

- 1 (3" x 3") square yellow solid
- 6 (3" x 3") squares red solid
- 12 (3" x 3") squares blue print
- ½ yard white solid
- ½ yard backing fabric
- Batting 20" x 20"
- Lining 20" x 20"

SUPPLIES & TOOLS

- Thread to match fabrics
- Freezer paper
- Glue stick
- 14" x 14" pillow form
- 1¼ yards red piping
- 3 (¾") buttons
- Zipper foot
- Basic sewing tools and supplies

Cutting

1. Cut one large hexagon white solid for A using pattern given on page 18.

2. Cut two B and two BR pieces white solid using the pattern given on page 17.

3. Using the 1" hexagon pattern given on page 17 and referring to the General Instructions, prepare one yellow solid, six red solid and 12 blue print hexagons.

4. Cut two 2½" x 10⅞" C strips white solid.

5. Cut two 2½" x 13½" D strips white solid.

6. Cut two 1¼" x 14⅞" E strips white solid.

7. Cut two 15" x 11" rectangles backing fabric.

Completing the Block

1. Referring to the General Instructions, complete one flower motif with a yellow center, first ring of red solid and final ring of blue print hexagons.

2. Fold the A hexagon in half vertically and horizontally and crease to mark centers.

3. Center the flower motif on A referring to Figure 1; machine-stitch in place referring to the General Instructions.

Figure 1

4. Trim backing away from behind appliqué motif and remove papers referring to the General Instructions.

5. Trim the piping seam allowance to ¼" as shown in Figure 2. Cut six 7" pieces of piping.

Figure 2

6. Align the piping pieces on the side edges of the block; pin to hold.

7. Using a zipper foot, sew as close to the piping as possible, overlapping ends at the corners as shown in Figure 3; trim excess piping at ends.

Figure 3

8. Sew B and BR to the sides of the appliquéd center to complete the block.

Completing the Top
1. Sew C to the top and bottom of the block; press seams toward C.

2. Sew D to opposite sides of the pieced center; press seams toward D.

3. Sew an E strip to the top and bottom of the pieced center; press seams toward E.

Finishing the Pillow
1. Sandwich batting between the completed top and the prepared lining piece; pin or baste layers together.

2. Quilt as desired by hand or machine. When quilting is complete, trim edges even; remove pins or basting.

3. Fold one 15" end under ¼" on each pillow backing rectangle; press. Fold over 1¾" again; press and stitch to hem.

Figure 4   **Figure 5**

4. Evenly space and stitch three buttonholes ¾" from folded edge of one hemmed backing piece as shown in Figure 4.

5. Overlap backing pieces with the buttonhole piece on top referring to Figure 5; baste overlapping layers together.

6. Sew a button beneath each buttonhole on the underneath backing piece.

7. Place the basted backing pieces right sides together with the pillow top; stitch all around pillow. Turn right side out through the back opening. Insert pillow form. ∎

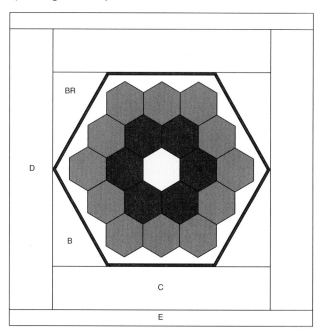

Vintage Garden Pillow
Placement Diagram
14⅜" x 14½"

Simply Orchids

The beauty of the orchid lies in its simple and elegant lines in this wall quilt and pillow set.

PROJECT SPECIFICATIONS
Skill Level: Beginner
Quilt Size: 21" x 38"
Pillow Size: 16" x 20"
Block Size: 10" x 14"
Templates Used: 1" hexagon

FABRIC & BATTING
- Scraps purple variegated batik
- ⅛ yard green print
- ⅛ yard medium green mottled
- ¼ yard multicolored batik
- ⅓ yard gold mottled
- ½ yard blue mottled
- ½ yard coordinating fabric for pillow backing
- 1 yard dark brown mottled
- Backing 27" x 44"
- Batting 27" x 44" and 18" x 22"
- Pillow lining 18" x 22"

SUPPLIES & TOOLS
- Thread to match fabrics
- Clear monofilament
- Freezer paper
- Glue stick
- 16" x 20" purchased or self-made pillow form
- Basic sewing tools and supplies

Cutting
1. Cut four 8½" x 12½" A rectangles blue mottled.

2. Cut four 2½" x 8½" B strips brown mottled.

3. Cut two 2⅞" x 2⅞" squares brown mottled;

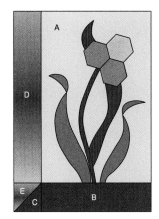

Simply Orchid
10" x 14" Block

cut each square on one diagonal to make four C triangles.

4. Cut four 2½" x 12½" D strips multicolored batik.

5. Cut two 2⅞" x 2⅞" squares multicolored batik; cut each square on one diagonal to make four E triangles.

6. Cut four 1" x 14½" F strips and two 1" x 32½" G strips gold mottled.

7. Cut two 3½" x 15½" H strips and two 3½" x 38½" I strips brown mottled.

8. Cut two 1" x 10½" J strips and two 1" x 15½" K strips gold mottled.

9. Cut two 3" x 11½" L strips and two 3" x 20½" M strips brown mottled.

10. Prepare templates for appliquéd leaves and

stems using patterns given. Cut shapes from fabrics as directed on each piece, adding ⅛"–¼" seam allowance all around each piece when cutting.

11. Prepare four gold mottled and eight purple variegated batik flower petals using the 1" hexagon pattern on page 18 and referring to the General Instructions.

12. Cut two 16½" x 13" rectangles pillow backing fabric.

13. Cut three 2¼" by fabric width strips brown mottled for binding.

Completing the Blocks
1. Turn under edges of leaf and stem pieces; glue-baste to hold.

2. Arrange prepared leaf and stem shapes on A, referring to the pattern for positioning, matching the ends of the pieces with the bottom edge of A.

3. Machine-stitch shapes in place using clear monofilament and a small zigzag stitch.

4. Join one gold and two purple variegated flower petals referring to the General Instructions; repeat. Repeat with one purple variegated and two gold mottled petals for one flower and three purple variegated petals for the final flower.

5. Appliqué a flower unit on A over the leaf and stem ends referring to the Placement Diagram and pattern for positioning.

6. Sew B to the bottom of each stitched unit; press seams toward B.

7. Sew C to E along the diagonal; press seam toward E. Repeat for four units.

8. Sew a C-E unit to the end of D, matching the E end of the C-E unit to the end of D as shown in Figure 1; press seams toward D.

Figure 1

9. Sew a D-C-E strip to the left side edge of the stitched unit. Repeat for four blocks.

Completing the Wall Quilt Top
1. Join three blocks with four F strips; press seams toward F.

2. Sew a G strip to the top and bottom of the pieced center; press seams toward G.

3. Sew an H strip to opposite short ends and I strips to the top and bottom of the pieced center; press seams toward H and I strips.

Completing the Pillow Top
1. Sew a J strip to the top and bottom and K strip to opposite sides of the remaining block; press seams toward J and K.

2. Sew an L strip to the top and bottom and M strips to opposite sides of the remaining block; press seams toward L and M.

Simply Orchids Wall Quilt
Placement Diagram
21" x 38"

Finishing the Wall Quilt

1. Sandwich the 27" x 44" batting piece between the same-size backing and the wall quilt top; pin or baste layers to hold.

2. Quilt as desired by hand or machine. When quilting is complete, trim edges even; remove pins or basting.

3. Join binding strips on short ends to make one long strip; press seams open. Pin binding to the right side of the quilted top, aligning raw edges. Stitch all around, mitering corners and overlapping ends.

4. Turn the binding to the wrong side; hand- or machine-stitch in place to finish.

Finishing the Pillow

1. Sandwich the 18" x 22" batting between the same-size pillow lining piece and the pillow top; pin or baste layers to hold.

2. Quilt as desired by hand or machine. When quilting is complete, trim edges even; remove pins or basting.

3. Fold one 16½" end under ¼" on each pillow backing rectangle; press. Fold under ½" again; press and stitch to hem.

4. Place the hemmed backing pieces right sides together with the quilted pillow top, overlapping pieces in the center referring to Figure 2; baste overlapping layers together.

Figure 2

5. Stitch all around pillow. Turn right side out through the back opening. Insert pillow form. ■

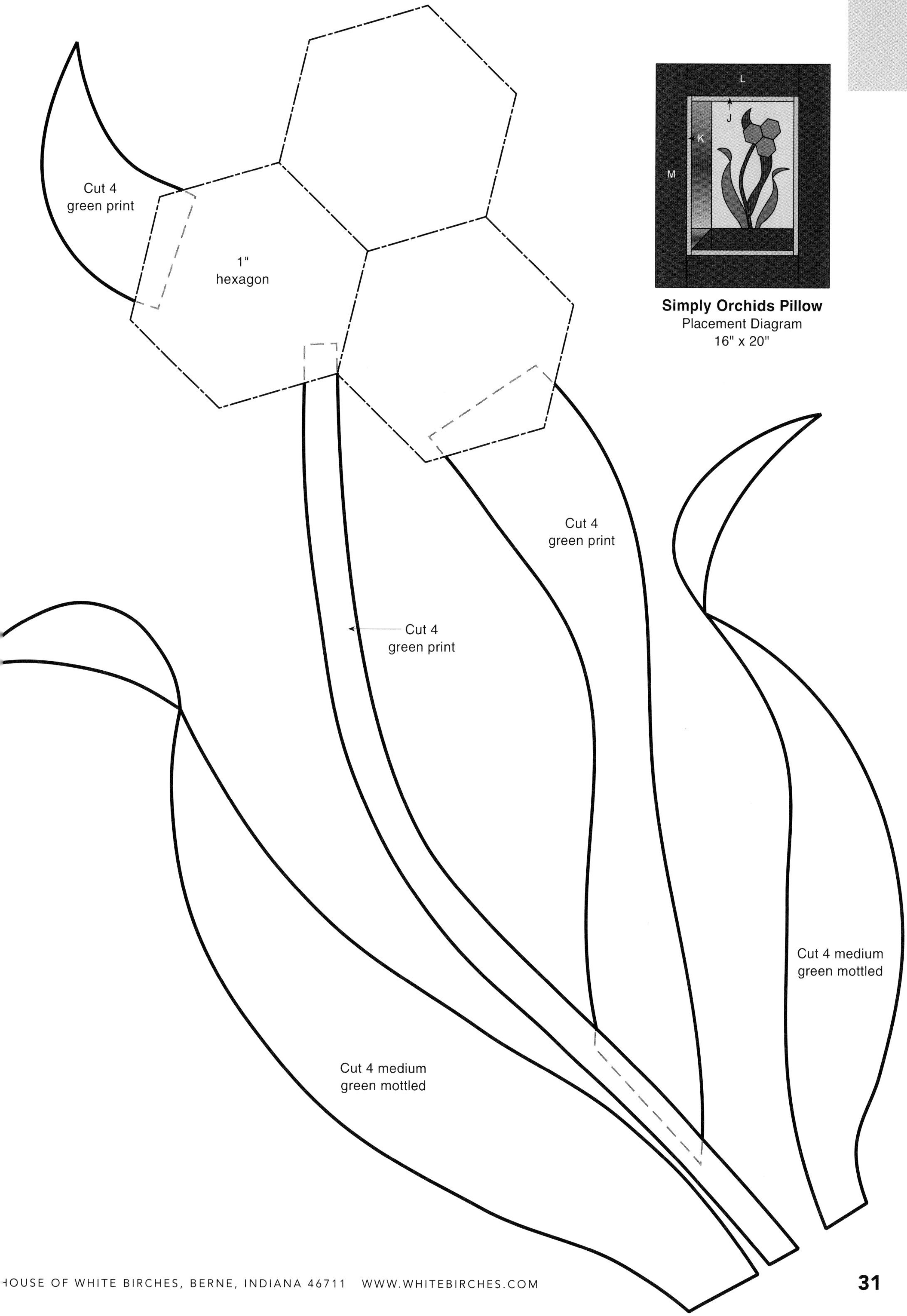

Cut 4
green print

1"
hexagon

Simply Orchids Pillow
Placement Diagram
16" x 20"

L

J

K

M

Cut 4
green print

Cut 4
green print

Cut 4 medium
green mottled

Cut 4 medium
green mottled

Pioneer Poppies

Try piecing and appliqué to make this small wall quilt.

PROJECT SPECIFICATIONS
Skill Level: Intermediate
Quilt Size: 25" x 25"
Block Size: 7" x 7"
Number of Blocks: 4
Templates Used: 1" hexagon and 1" diamond

FABRIC & BATTING
- ⅛ yard red check
- 1 fat quarter rose print
- ¼ yard black print
- ¼ yard white print
- ¼ yard black-and-white print
- ¼ yard black solid
- Backing 31" x 31"
- Batting 31" x 31"

SUPPLIES & TOOLS
- Thread to match fabrics
- Freezer paper
- Glue stick
- 4 yards black ¼"-wide fusible bias tape
- Water-erasable marker or pencil
- Basic sewing tools and supplies

Cutting
1. Cut 24 rose print and four black print flower petals using the 1" hexagon pattern on page 17.

2. Cut eight rose print diamonds using the 1" diamond pattern on page 16.

3. Cut four 7¾" x 7¾" A squares white print.

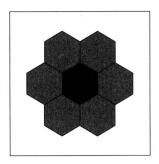

Poppy
7" x 7" Block

4. Cut six 1½" x 7½" B strips and three 1½" x 17½" C strips black print.

5. Cut two 1" x 17½" D strips and two 1" x 18½" E strips red check.

6. Cut two 4" x 18½" F strips and two 4" x 25½" G strips black-and-white print

7. Cut three 2¼" by fabric width strips black solid for binding.

Completing the Blocks
1. Prepare four flower motifs with black print centers and rose print petals referring to the General Instructions.

2. Fold and crease each A square to mark the horizontal and vertical centers.

3. Center a flower motif on one A square, aligning the seam between two petals with the vertical center creases as shown in Figure 1;

machine-stitch in place referring to the General Instructions.

Figure 1

4. Trim block to 7½" x 7½" square. Repeat for four Poppy blocks.

5. Trim backing away and remove freezer-paper pieces referring to the General Instructions.

Completing the Top

1. Join two blocks with three B strips to make a row; press seams toward B. Repeat for two rows.

2. Join the block rows with three C strips; press seams toward C.

3. Sew a D strip to the top and bottom and an E strip to opposite sides of the pieced center; press seams toward D and E.

4. Sew an F strip to the top and bottom and a G strip to opposite sides of the pieced center; press seams toward F and G.

5. Prepare a template for the curving border design, using the pattern given.

6. Transfer the curving border design to the F and G borders referring to the Placement Diagram for positioning.

7. Place the black ¼"-wide fusible bias tape along the marked lines, fusing as you go.

8. Arrange a 1" rose diamond inside each inverted point of bias tape, referring to the Placement Diagram for positioning.

9. Using thread to match fabrics, machine-stitch diamond shapes and bias tape in place.

Finishing the Quilt

1. Sandwich batting between the completed top and the prepared backing piece; pin or baste layers together.

2. Quilt as desired by hand or machine. When quilting is complete, trim edges even; remove pins or basting.

3. Using black thread, stitch along each side of the fused bias tape.

4. Join binding strips on short ends to make one long strip; press seams open. Pin binding to the right side of the quilted top, aligning raw edges. Stitch all around, mitering corners and overlapping ends.

5. Turn the binding to the wrong side; hand- or machine-stitch in place to finish. ■

Pioneer Poppies
Placement Diagram
25" x 25"

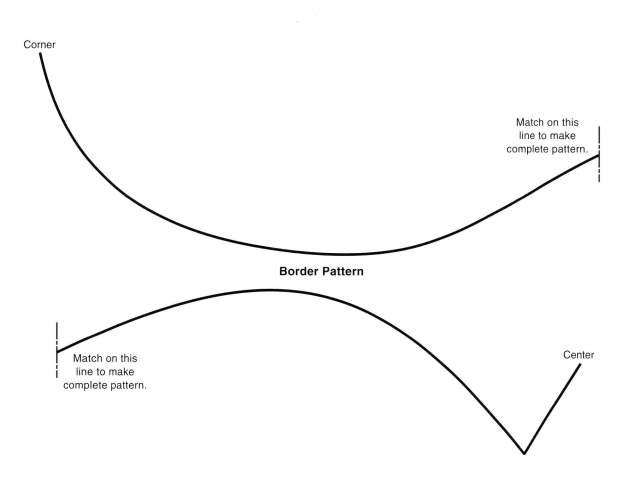

Corner

Match on this line to make complete pattern.

Border Pattern

Match on this line to make complete pattern.

Center

Grape Harvest

Hexagon shapes can be used to make many different designs. This quilt uses them to make basket shapes and grape clusters.

PROJECT SPECIFICATIONS
Skill Level: Advanced
Quilt Size: 60" x 60"
Block Size: 10" x 10"
Number of Blocks: 9
Templates Used: ½" and 1" hexagons

FABRIC & BATTING
- 3 fat quarters green solids and/or prints
- ⅛ yard purple solid
- ¼ yard total reddish and golden brown scraps (baskets and stems)
- ⅓ yard total purple, reddish purple and blue scraps (grapes)
- ⅜ yard brown plaid
- ¾ yard purple plaid
- 1⅝ yards brown solid
- 2¾ yards cream tonal
- Backing 66" x 66"
- Batting 66" x 66"

SUPPLIES & TOOLS
- Thread to match fabrics
- Freezer paper
- Glue stick
- 8 yards ⅜"-wide fusible tape
- Basic sewing tools and supplies

Cutting
1. Referring to Figure 1, cut nine 11" x 11" A squares, eight 2¼" by fabric width F strips, eight 2½" x 5¾" H strips, two 7" x 47½" L strips and two 7" x 60½" M strips cream tonal.

Basket Block
10" x 10" Block

Grape Cluster
10" x 10" Block

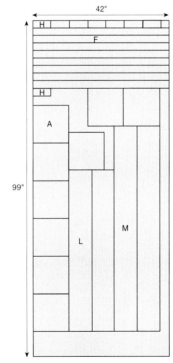

Figure 1

2. Cut two 10½" by fabric width strips purple plaid; subcut strips into (24) 2½" B strips.

3. Cut one 2½" by fabric width strip purple solid; subcut strip into (16) 2½" C squares.

4. Cut two 1½" x 38½" D strips and two 1½" x 40½" E strips brown solid.

5. Cut four 2¼" by fabric width G strips brown plaid.

6. Cut four 3" x 3" I squares brown solid.

7. Cut five 1½" by fabric width strips brown solid. Join strips on short ends to make one long strip; subcut strip into two 45½" J strips and two 47½" K strips.

8. Prepare (45) 1" brown-scrap hexagons referring to the General Instructions.

9. Prepare (76) ½" purple/blue-scrap hexagons referring to the General Instructions.

10. Cut ¾"-wide strips brown solid bias to total 280".

11. Prepare templates for stem and leaf pieces using patterns given; cut as directed on each piece.

12. Cut seven 2¼" by fabric width strips brown solid for binding.

Completing the Basket Blocks

1. Fold each A square vertically and horizontally and crease to mark the center; set aside four A squares for Grape Cluster blocks.

2. Refer to the General Instructions to join seven prepared brown-scrap hexagons to make a flower; add two additional hexagons to make the basket shape referring to Figure 2.

Figure 2

3. Center the top of the basket shape along the horizontal crease of one A square as shown in Figure 3; pin to hold.

Figure 3

4. Join ¾"-wide bias strips on short ends to make a long strip. Press seams open. Fold under ⅛"–¼" on each long edge to make ⅜"-wide bias; press. Bond ⅜"-wide fusible tape to the wrong side.

5. Cut a 12" length of ⅜"-wide fused brown bias for basket handle; remove paper backing.

6. Arrange the bias in a curve over the pinned basket shape, starting with one end at the tip of the top outside hexagon and ending at the top of the outside hexagon on the opposite side, tucking ends under basket shape; fuse in place.

7. Machine-stitch the basket shape and handle in place referring to the General Instructions.

8. Trim the background away from behind the

stitched basket shape and remove freezer-paper pieces referring to the General Instructions.

9. Trim square to 10½" x 10½" to complete one Basket block; repeat for five blocks.

Completing the Grape Cluster Blocks

1. Refer to the General Instructions to join seven prepared purple/blue hexagons to make a flower; add four additional hexagons to make the grape cluster shape referring to Figure 4. ***Note: Grape clusters do not have to have the same configuration or shape.***

Figure 4

2. Pin a stem, two leaf shapes and one grape cluster to each A square, centering the motif on the square.

3. Machine-stitch pieces in place referring to the General Instructions.

4. Trim the stitched square to 10½" x 10½" to complete one block; repeat for four blocks.

Completing the Top

1. Join one Grape Cluster block with two Basket blocks and four B strips to make a block row as shown in Figure 5; press seams toward B strips. Repeat for two rows.

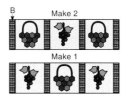

Figure 5

2. Join one Basket block with two Grape Cluster blocks and four B strips to make a block row, again referring to Figure 5; press seams toward B strips.

3. Join three B strips with four C squares to make a sashing row; press seams toward B. Repeat for four sashing rows.

4. Join the block rows with the sashing rows to complete the pieced center; press seams toward sashing rows.

5. Sew a D strip to opposite sides and an E strip to the top and bottom of the pieced center; press seams toward D and E.

6. Sew a G strip between two F strips with right sides together along length; press seams toward G. Repeat for four strip sets. Subcut strip sets into (64) 2¼" F-G units as shown in Figure 6.

Figure 6

7. Join 16 F-G units, staggering units as shown in Figure 7; press seams in one direction. Repeat for four 16-unit strips.

Figure 7

11. Sew an F-G-H strip to opposite sides of the pieced center; press seams toward D strips. Sew an I square to each end of each remaining F-G-H strip; press seams toward I. Sew these strips to the top and bottom of the pieced center; press seams toward E.

12. Sew a J strip to opposite sides and K strips to the top and bottom of the pieced center; press seams toward J and K strips.

13. Sew an L strip to opposite sides and M strips to the top and bottom of the pieced center; press seams toward L and M strips.

14. Arrange the remaining ³⁄₈" fused bias strip on the L and M strips to create a flowing curve that is rounded at the corners referring to Figure 11. When satisfied with positioning, fuse in place.

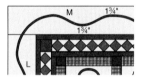

Figure 11

15. Join four prepared grapes to make a small cluster as shown in Figure 12. Repeat for eight clusters in varying arrangements.

Figure 12

16. Arrange and pin one cluster at each corner and at each border center referring to the Placement Diagram. When satisfied with positioning, machine-appliqué clusters in place.

17. Arrange and pin leaf shapes around the fused bias with two leaves with each grape cluster and three between center and corners referring to the Placement Diagram for positioning. When satisfied with positioning, machine-appliqué shapes in place to complete the top.

8. Sew an H strip to each end of each strip as shown in Figure 8.

Figure 8

9. Trim each strip ¼" beyond the G points to make 3"-wide strips as shown in Figure 9.

Figure 9

10. Trim each F-G-H strip square at each end as shown in Figure 10 to make 3" x 40½" strips.

Figure 10

Finishing the Wall Quilt

1. Sandwich the batting between the prepared backing and the completed top; pin or baste layers to hold.

2. Quilt as desired by hand or machine; trim edges even and remove pins or basting.

3. Join binding strips on short ends to make one long strip; press seams open. Pin binding to the right side of the quilted top, aligning raw edges. Stitch all around, mitering corners and overlapping ends.

4. Turn the binding to the wrong side; hand- or machine-stitch in place to finish. ∎

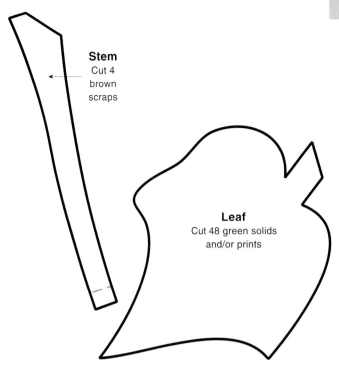

Stem
Cut 4
brown
scraps

Leaf
Cut 48 green solids
and/or prints

Grape Harvest
Placement Diagram
60" x 60"

Froggy's Flower Garden

Have fun creating a fabric flower garden in a little pond for the froggies to play in.

PROJECT NOTES

Use scraps of various brights, tiny motif prints, darks and an assortment of greens (stripe, check, prints) and a lot of interesting textures and designs for the hexagons. Bugs, spiders, fish or frogs may be fussy-cut and added as desired. This little quilt is fun to stitch, and children will love to find the interesting creatures hiding all over it.

PROJECT SPECIFICATIONS

Skill Level: Intermediate
Quilt Size: 16" x 21"
Template Used: ½" hexagon

FABRIC & BATTING

- Scraps fish, lizard or snake prints with 1"–1½" motifs for fussy cutting
- 6 (2"-long) frog motifs
- 1 fat quarter mottled water fabric for background
- 1 fat quarter coordinating border print
- ⅛ yard fuchsia tonal
- ¼ yard total scraps to make hexagons
- ¼ yard aqua mottled for binding
- Backing 22" x 27"
- Batting 22" x 27"

SUPPLIES & TOOLS

- Thread to match fabrics
- Freezer paper
- Glue stick
- ¼ yard fusible web
- Basic sewing tools and supplies

Cutting

1. Bond fusible web to the wrong side of the frog motifs; cut around shapes, leaving ¹⁄₁₆" extra around edge. Remove paper backing. Set aside one frog motif for stuffing later.

2. Cut one 1" x 18" B strip and one 1" x 16" C strip fuchsia tonal.

3. Cut one 5½" x 17¼" D strip coordinating border print.

4. Cut two 2½" x 14½" E strips and two 2½" x 21½" F strips coordinating border print.

5. Cut hexagons for seven single flowers from scraps using one center fabric and six petal fabrics for each flower using the ½" hexagon pattern given on page 17 and referring to the General Instructions. **Note:** *The sample shown has bugs centered in some of the flowers.*

6. Referring to Making 3-D Flowers on page 50, prepare one 3-D flower from scraps, using the ½" hexagon pattern. Use contrasting fabrics for the top, lining fabics for the 3-D petals, and green for the six base petals. **Note**: *See Fussy Cutting in the General Instructions to hide something under the 3-D flower.*

7. Referring to the General Instructions, prepare at least 31 green scrap ½" hexagons to use as connectors to fill in the background around the

flowers. **Note:** *It is a good idea to prepare extra hexagons so you can pick and choose when you are composing the hexagon background around the flowers.*

8. Cut three 2¼" by fabric width strips aqua mottled for binding.

Completing the Top

1. Prepare seven single flowers and one 3-D flower referring to the General Instructions.

2. Arrange the 3-D and hexagon flowers on the fat-quarter background piece, referring to the Placement Diagram for positioning.

3. Fill in the area between the flowers with the connector hexagons to create a water garden. When satisfied with the arrangement, piece together the whole thing as one unit. **Note**: *It is easiest to start in the center. You may leave spaces in between the hexagons to allow the background to show through.*

4. Pin the garden unit to the fat-quarter background ¾" from the left side edge and 1"

from the bottom edge. Place five fused frog shapes where desired around the water garden, tucking the edge of the shapes underneath the garden as necessary. When satisfied with positioning, fuse shapes in place.

5. Machine-appliqué around all edges of the water garden and in any holes you have left; repeat with frog shapes.

6. Trim away fabric from behind appliquéd shapes and remove freezer-paper pieces referring to the General Instructions.

7. Trim the right and top edges of the background to leave a 14" x 17" rectangle for A as shown in Figure 1.

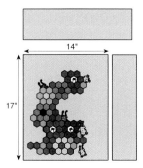

Figure 1   **Figure 2**

8. Sew B to the left side edge and C to the top edge of A, mitering corner. Trim seam allowance to ¼" at corner; press mitered seam open and border seams toward B and C.

9. Lay the D strip right side up on the right edge of the fused top with outer edges aligned; cut the inside edge of D in a curving design that is pleasing to you referring to the photo of the quilt and Figure 2.

10. Turn under the inside edge and hand- or machine-appliqué in place.

11. Sew an E strip to the top and bottom and the F strip to the left side of the pieced center to complete the pieced top.

Finishing the Quilt

1. Sandwich the batting between the prepared backing and the completed top; pin or baste layers to hold.

2. Quilt as desired by hand or machine; trim edges even and remove pins or basting. ***Note****: Be sure to pull the petals up on the 3-D flower so they won't get quilted into the background.*

3. Join binding strips on short ends to make one long strip; press seams open. Pin binding to the right side of the quilted top, aligning raw edges. Stitch all around, mitering corners and overlapping ends.

4. Turn the binding to the wrong side; hand- or machine-stitch in place to finish. ▪

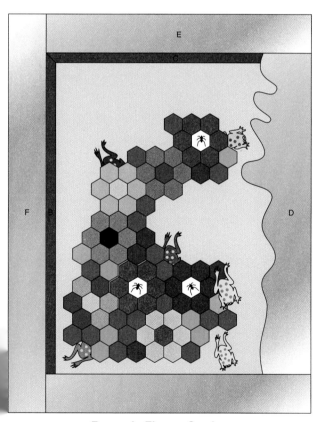

Froggy's Flower Garden
Placement Diagram
16" x 21"

Adding a 3-D Frog

Use the remaining frog motif to make a 3-D frog to attach to your top.

You need a scrap of fabric for the frog lining a little larger than the frog. Bond fusible web to the back of this fabric.

Pin the frog motif (with fusible web already trimmed) to the frog lining fabric, with fusible sides together.

Using the frog motif as a template, cut out the same shape from the frog lining fabric; remove paper from both pieces and put back together with fusible sides together.

Place a small piece of batting or stuffing (you may use what is trimmed from the quilt) between the two pieces as shown in Figure 3 (be sure you have a little space around the edges of the frog so the edges of the fabric will fuse together). Fuse together around the edge of the frog.

Batting

Figure 3

Stitch around the edges of the frog for added stability. Tack the stuffed frog to the top of the quilt.

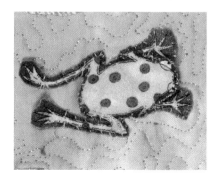

Purple Haze on Summer Daze

Pretty 3-D flowers are surrounded by a picket fence in this perky summertime quilt.

PROJECT SPECIFICATIONS

Skill Level: Intermediate
Quilt Size: 68" x 83"
Block Size: 8½" x 8½"
Number of Blocks: 22
Templates Used: 1" and 1½" hexagons

FABRIC & BATTING

- ⅝ yard lavender stripe
- ⅞ yard yellow print
- 1¼ yards lavender print
- 1¾ yards green mottled
- 2 yards white plaid
- 2⅜ yards green floral
- Backing 74" x 89"
- Batting 74" x 89"

SUPPLIES & TOOLS

- Thread to match fabrics
- Freezer paper
- Glue stick
- Basic sewing tools and supplies

Cutting

1. Using the 1½" hexagon pattern given on page 17 and referring to the General Instructions, prepare 22 yellow print 1½" hexagons for the flower centers and 132 lavender print 1½" hexagons for the base petals.

2. Using the 1" hexagon pattern given on page 17 and referring to the General Instructions, cut

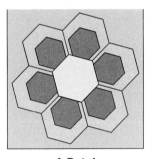

A Petal
8½" x 8½" Block

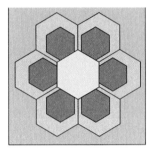

J Petal
8½" x 8½" Block

132 lavender stripe hexagons for the 3-D petal tops and 132 yellow print for the 3-D petal linings.

3. Cut five 9¼" by fabric width strips green mottled; subcut strips into (18) 9¼" A squares.

4. Cut three 9" by fabric width strips white plaid; subcut strips into (48) 2½" B sashing strips.

5. Cut two 2½" by fabric width strips lavender print; subcut strips into (31) 2½" C squares.

6. Cut three 16⅛" x 16⅛" squares green floral; cut each square on both diagonals to make 12 D triangles. Set aside two triangles for another project.

7. Cut two 9¾" x 9¾" squares green floral; cut each square on one diagonal to make four E triangles.

5. Trim block to 9" x 9" square. Repeat for 18 A Petal blocks.

6. Trim backing away and remove papers, referring to the General Instructions.

7. Fold each J square in half and crease horizontal and vertical centers.

8. Center a flower motif on J, aligning seams with vertical crease as shown in Figure 2.

Figure 2

9. Complete four J Petal blocks, referring to steps 4–6.

Completing the Top

1. Arrange the A Petal blocks in diagonal rows with the B sashing strips, C sashing squares, and D and E triangles, referring to Figure 3.

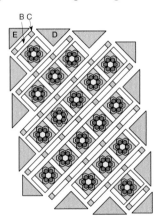

Figure 3

2. Join the blocks with B and D in diagonal rows; press seams toward B. Join B and C to make rows; press seams toward B.

3. Join the block rows and sashing rows, adding E triangles at corners to complete the pieced center; press seams in one direction.

8. Cut six 2¼" by fabric width strips white plaid. Join strips on short ends to make one long strip; subcut strip into two 63" F strips and two 51½" G strips.

9. Cut 12 strips each 2" by fabric width white plaid (H) and green floral (I).

10. Cut six 3½" by fabric width strips green floral. Join strips on short ends to make one long strip; subcut strip into two 66½" K strips and two 51½" L strips.

11. Cut four 9¼" x 9¼" J squares green floral.

12. Cut eight 2¼" by fabric width strips green floral for binding.

Completing Flower Blocks

1. Refer to the General Instructions and Making 3-D Flowers on page 50 to complete 22 flowers.

2. Fold each A square on both diagonals and crease.

3. Align the seams of one flower motif on the diagonal creases of one A square as shown in Figure 1.

Figure 1

4. Machine-appliqué flower in place referring to the General Instructions.

4. Sew F strips to opposite long sides and G strips to the top and bottom of the pieced center; press seams toward F and G.

5. Join four each H and I strips with right sides together along length, alternating colors; press seams toward H. Repeat for three strip sets; subcut strip sets into (20) 6" segments as shown in Figure 4.

Figure 4

6. Join six H-I units to make a long strip; remove two H and two I strips from one end of the strip as shown in Figure 5; repeat for two strips.

Figure 5

7. Sew a K strip to one long side of each pieced strip; press seams toward K. Sew these strips to opposite long sides of the pieced center; press seams toward F strips.

8. Join four H-I units to make a long strip; repeat for two strips. Add one each H and I strips removed from previous strips to one end of each strip as shown in Figure 6. Sew an L strip to one long side of each pieced strip; press seams toward L strips.

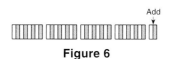

Figure 6

9. Sew a J Petal block to each end of each strip; press seams toward blocks. Sew a strip to the top and bottom of the pieced center to complete the pieced top; press seams toward G.

Finishing the Quilt

1. Sandwich batting between the completed top and the prepared backing piece; pin or baste layers together.

2. Quilt as desired by hand or machine. When quilting is complete, trim edges even; remove pins or basting. ***Note:*** *The quilt shown was machine-quilted, leaving the 3-D hexagon petals loose.*

3. Join binding strips on short ends to make one long strip; press seams open. Pin binding to the right side of the quilted top, aligning raw edges. Stitch all around, mitering corners and overlapping ends.

4. Turn the binding to the wrong side; hand- or machine-stitch in place to finish. ∎

Purple Haze on Summer Daze
Placement Diagram
68" x 83"

Making 3-D Flowers

Making flowers with stand-up 3-D petals is easy and gives you another design option when creating your quilts.

For each 3-D flower, you need seven templates for the flower center and base petals. The center and base petals are prepared referring to the General Instructions. You will need six additional freezer-paper templates for the 3-D petals, which may be reused five or six times.

Each 3-D petal is made with a top fabric and a lining fabric. These can be the same fabric or contrasting fabrics.

Cutting the 3-D Petals & Linings

1. Prepare freezer-paper templates using the template specified for the design referring to the General Instructions.

2. Place the petal top fabric and lining fabrics right sides together; press.

3. Place the freezer-paper templates on the wrong side of the layered fabric as in the General Instructions; press in place.

4. Place a pin through each template through both layers of fabric.

5. Cut ¼" away from the edge of the freezer-paper template through both layers of fabric.

Construction of the 3-D Flower

1. Decrease the machine-stitch length slightly. Sew around five sides of the layered petal units using the freezer-paper templates as guides, leaving one side open as shown in Figure 1.

Figure 1

2. Remove the freezer-paper template; trim seams and turn the petal unit right side out through the opening to complete one petal unit as shown in Figure 2; press.

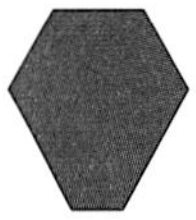

Figure 2

3. Repeat steps 1 and 2 to complete the required number of petal units.

Flower Construction

Note: *The assumption is that the base flower units have been cut and prepared for stitching already.*

1. Start with the base flower center hexagon right side up on a flat surface. Pin a petal unit on top of the base flower center with the raw edge of the petal unit extending ¼" beyond the folded-and-pressed edge of the base flower center as shown in Figure 3.

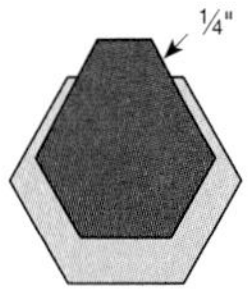

Figure 3

2. Place a base flower petal right sides together with the pinned unit, aligning edges with the base flower center as shown in Figure 4. *Note: You will now have a layer consisting of four pieces of fabric and two pieces of freezer paper.*

Paper

Paper

Figure 4   **Figure 5**

3. Machine zigzag-stitch along the edge of the base flower pieces and through the unfinished edge of the petal unit as shown in Figure 5.

4. Open the stitched unit; give it a tug. Do not cut the thread or remove the flower from the sewing machine. Move the flower to the left and add the next petal unit and base flower unit. Continue around all edges of the flower center.

5. Join base flower petals as in the General Instructions. *Note: Stitch only the sides of the base petals together, being careful not to catch the petal unit in the stitching.*

6. When flower units are complete, trim excess seam allowance off the inner edge of the petal units and remove paper patterns.

7. Treat the 3-D flowers the same as regular flowers after they have been constructed. ◼

The Purple Haze quilt has 3-D petals on each flower motif.

High Class Cubes

This is my high-class, high-rise chicken coop. You can see chickens in some of the windows with a little chicken feed scattered around, too.

PROJECT NOTES

This easy wall quilt plays with the value of fabrics and uses a 60-degree diamond as the template. In another life, this design is known as Tumbling Blocks. The inner yellow borders are a little funky (two different sizes) and the quilt was sewn with clear monofilament. Red piping sets off the mitered outside border. Although fussy cutting was not used here, it would be a perfect pattern to use. Let's see what's in your windows.

PROJECT SPECIFICATIONS

Skill Level: Beginner
Quilt Size: 28" x 33"
Template Used: 3" diamond

FABRIC & BATTING

- 9 (4" x 6") rectangles each light, medium and dark fabrics
- ¼ yard bright yellow solid
- ½ yard black-and-white stripe
- 1 yard black solid
- Backing 34" x 39"
- Batting 34" x 39"

SUPPLIES & TOOLS

- Thread to match fabrics
- Clear monofilament
- 1 package red piping
- Freezer paper
- Glue stick
- Basic sewing tools and supplies

Instructions

1. Cut a 20½" x 25½" A background rectangle black solid.

2. Cut one 1½" x 25" B strip, one 1" x 25" C strip, one 1½" x 21½" D strip and one 1" x 21½" E strip yellow solid.

3. Cut two 4" x 32" G strips and two 4" x 37" F strips black-and-white stripe.

4. Cut four 2¼" by fabric width strips black solid for binding.

Preparing Diamond Pieces

1. Using the 3" diamond template given on page 16, prepare nine diamonds each from the light, medium and dark fabric rectangles.

2. Referring to the instructions given for Tumbling Blocks Construction on page 56, arrange and join three diamonds to make a block; repeat for nine blocks.

3. Join the blocks in rows and join the rows, making sure to correctly place the light, medium and dark pieces referring to Figure 1 to create the optical illusion.

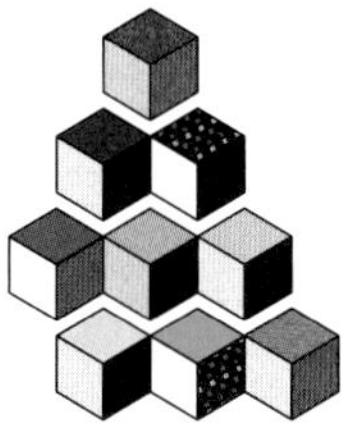

Figure 1

Completing the Top

1. Referring to Figure 2, place the stitched diamond unit on A; hand-baste or glue-baste to hold. Machine-appliqué in place using clear monofilament.

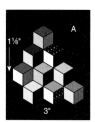

Figure 2

2. Referring to the General Instructions, trim the background from under the appliqué area and remove paper templates.

3. Press and trim A to 20" x 25".

4. Referring to the Placement Diagram for positioning, sew B to one 25" side and C to the other 25" side of the appliquéd center; press seams toward B and C.

5. Sew D to the bottom and E to the top of the appliquéd center; press seams toward D and E.

6. Center and sew an F strip to opposite sides and G strips to the top and bottom of the appliquéd center, stopping stitching at the end of the seam allowance and mitering corners. Trim excess seam at miter to ¼"; press mitered seams open. Press remaining seams toward F and G.

Completing the Quilt

1. Sandwich batting between the completed top and the prepared backing piece; pin or baste layers together.

2. Quilt as desired by hand or machine. When quilting is complete, trim edges even; remove pins or basting. **Note:** *The quilt shown was machine-quilted in the ditch around all of the diamonds using clear monofilament. Phantom*

diamonds were stitched in the open areas of the A background using the diamond template. The outer borders and remaining background were stipple-quilted by machine.

3. Trim the piping seam allowance to ¼" as shown in Figure 3. Cut two 30" and two 35" pieces piping.

Figure 3

4. Align the 35" piping pieces with the side edges of the appliquéd top and the 30" pieces with top and bottom, overlapping ends at corners as shown in Figure 4; pin to hold.

Figure 4

5. Using a zipper foot, sew as close to the piping as possible as shown in Figure 5; trim excess piping at ends.

Figure 5

6. Join binding strips on short ends to make one long strip; press seams open. Pin binding to the right side of the quilted top, aligning raw edges. Stitch all around, mitering corners and overlapping ends. **Note:** *If you sew the binding on from the back side of the quilt, you can follow the stitching line for adding the piping.*

7. Turn the binding to the wrong side; hand- or machine-stitch in place to finish. ■

High-Class Cubes
Placement Diagram
28" x 33"

Tumbling Blocks Construction

Tumbling blocks are made using 60-degree diamonds. For each block you must prepare three diamonds. Use the large diamond pattern and freezer paper. Prepare the pieces using glue basting, as for hexagons (refer to the General Instructions). However, for diamonds, I find it helps to trim the top and bottom points off the diamond as shown in Figure 1, leaving approximately ⅛" to turn under.

Color is not as important as the change in value. Make sure to place all the lights facing the same way. It doesn't matter where you place them as long as they are placed in the same direction, which creates the illusion.

Photo 1 shows a prepared diamond shape and a completed Tumbling Block unit from the right and wrong sides.

Piecing Instructions

1. Glue-baste the trimmed ends first; then the four sides.

2. To achieve the 3-D illusion of Tumbling Blocks, choose one each light-, medium- and dark-valued fabric for each block.

3. Join the dark and medium diamond shapes referring to the General Instructions. (Photo 2)

Figure 1

Photo 1

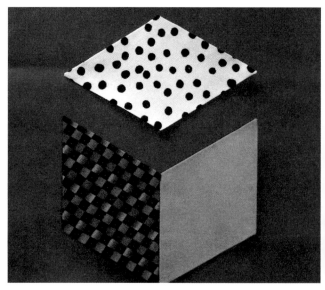

Photo 2

4. Place the light diamond shape on top of the dark diamond. (Photo 3)

Photo 3

5. Zigzag-stitch from the top point to the intersection in the center. (Photo 4) Stop stitching with needle in the zag position (off the fabric), grab the bottom point of the light diamond and pull it down and align with the medium diamond, matching edges, folding the dark diamond in half. (Photo 5)

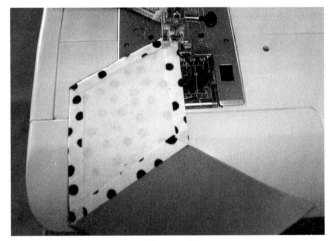
Photo 4

6. Continue zigzagging to the bottom point. Remove the block; press flat.

Photo 5

Connecting Units

1. Join block sides in a row. (Photo 6)

Photo 6

2. Set in remaining blocks one at a time, starting from the left and working your way to the right, folding the templates in order to make the Y seam as in piecing the blocks. ***Note:*** *Remember to make sure the blocks are facing the way you want them to by laying them out as they will be placed when they are stitched.* ◼

Stars Over Paris

Dream of a trip to Paris as you stitch this beautiful pastel-color quilt.

PROJECT SPECIFICATIONS
Skill Level: Beginner
Quilt Size: 49½" x 69"
Block Size: 8½" x 8½"
Number of Blocks: 18
Template Used: 1¾" Diamond

FABRIC & BATTING
- ¼ yard pink tonal
- ⅜ yard yellow tonal
- ¾ yard white tonal
- 1½ yards pink print
- 1⅝ yards white print
- 1¾ yards green tonal
- Backing 56" x 75"
- Batting 56" x 75"

SUPPLIES & TOOLS
- Thread to match fabrics
- Freezer paper
- Glue stick
- 18 white heart-shape buttons
- Basic sewing tools and supplies

Cutting
1. Cut three 7" by fabric width strips white tonal; subcut strips into (18) 7" x 7" A squares.

2. Cut five 5⅛" by fabric width strips green tonal; subcut strips into (36) 5⅛" squares.
Cut each square on one diagonal to make 72 B triangles.

3. Cut 54 total pink tonal and pink print and 54 yellow tonal 1¾" diamonds using pattern

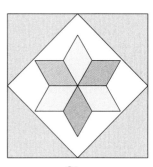

Star
8½" x 8½" Block

given on page 16 and referring to the General Instructions on page 6.

4. Cut four 3½" x 51½" C strips and two 3½" x 38" D strips along the length of the white print.

5. Cut six 6½" by fabric width strips pink print. Join strips on short ends to make one long strip. Subcut strip into two 57½" E and two 50" F strips.

6. Cut 2½"-wide green tonal bias strips to total 300" for binding.

Completing the Blocks
1. Fold A squares on both diagonals and crease to mark centers.

2. For each block, prepare three yellow diamonds and three pink diamonds referring to the General Instructions for hexagons and Tumbling Blocks Construction for diamonds.

3. To complete one star unit, join the diamond pieces, alternating colors, referring to Sixty-Degree Star Construction on page 63.

3. Sew a D strip to the top and bottom of the pieced center; press seams toward D strips.

4. Sew E strips to opposite sides and F strips to the top and bottom of the pieced center to complete the pieced top; press seams toward E and F strips.

Finishing the Wall Quilt
1. Sandwich the batting between the prepared backing and the completed top; pin or baste layers to hold.

2. Quilt as desired by hand or machine. When quilting is complete, trim edges even; remove pins or basting.

4. Center a star unit on the diagonal creases of one A square referring to Figure 1; machine-appliqué star units in place.

Figure 1

5. Trim the appliquéd A square to 6½" x 6½".

6. Sew a B triangle to each side of the appliquéd A square to complete one block; press seams toward B. Repeat to make 18 blocks.

7. Cut away fabric from behind the appliquéd star shapes and remove freezer-paper pieces referring to the General Instructions.

Completing the Top
1. Join six blocks to make a vertical row; press seams open. Repeat for three rows.

2. Join the rows with four C strips; press seams toward C strips.

Stars Over Paris
Placement Diagram
49½" x 69"

3. Mark three scallop patterns on each side of the center on each long side; mark two scallop patterns on each side of center on the top and bottom borders using pattern given and referring to Figure 2.

Figure 2

4. Fold quilt diagonally from corner to corner, mark the corner pattern on both sides of each corner as shown in Figure 3. Refold quilt and mark remaining two corners.

Figure 3

5. Trim around edge of quilt on marked scallop line.

6. Join binding strips on short ends to make one long strip; press seams open. Pin binding to the right side of the quilted top, aligning raw edges. Stitch all around, mitering corners and overlapping ends.

7. Turn the binding to the wrong side; hand- or machine-stitch in place.

8. Sew a heart-shape button to the center of each Star block to finish. ▪

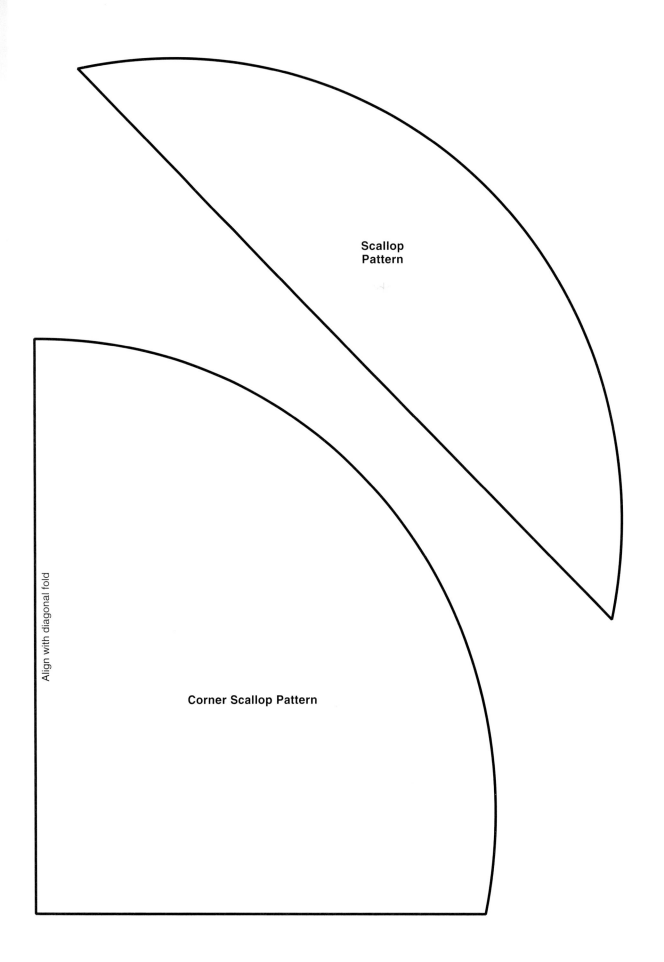

Scallop
Pattern

Align with diagonal fold

Corner Scallop Pattern

60-Degree Star Construction

The 60-degree diamond shape is used in several different sizes in a few of the projects in this book.

To prepare paper pieces, refer to Tumbling Blocks Construction on page 56. You will need six prepared diamonds for each star.

Divide the diamonds into two color families, make them all one color, fussy-cut them or even make them all different colors. Stars Over Paris uses yellow and pink, with more than one fabric in the pink colorway.

Piecing Instructions

1. To construct the star shape, lay the diamonds out in a star shape on a flat surface.

2. Start by joining two diamonds into a pair referring to Tumbling Blocks Construction; repeat for two pairs of diamonds. (Photo 1)

3. Attach a third diamond to each pair, creating two halves. (Photo 2)

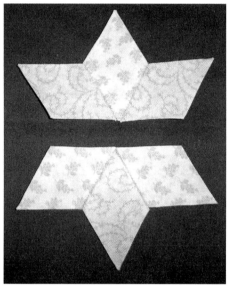

Photo 2

4. Join the two halves to complete a star unit. (Photo 3)

Photo 3

Photo 1

Metric Conversion Charts

Metric Conversions

U.S. Measurements		Multiplied by		Metric Measurement
yards	x	.9144	=	meters (m)
yards	x	91.44	=	centimeters (cm)
inches	x	2.54	=	centimeters (cm)
inches	x	25.40	=	millimeters (mm)
inches	x	.0254	=	meters (m)

Metric Measurements		Multiplied by		U.S. Measurements
centimeters	x	.3937	=	inches
meters	x	1.0936	=	yards

Standard Equivalents

U.S. Measurement		Metric Measurement		
1/8 inch	=	3.20 mm	=	0.32 cm
1/4 inch	=	6.35 mm	=	0.635 cm
3/8 inch	=	9.50 mm	=	0.95 cm
1/2 inch	=	12.70 mm	=	1.27 cm
5/8 inch	=	15.90 mm	=	1.59 cm
3/4 inch	=	19.10 mm	=	1.91 cm
7/8 inch	=	22.20 mm	=	2.22 cm
1 inch	=	25.40 mm	=	2.54 cm
1/8 yard	=	11.43 cm	=	0.11 m
1/4 yard	=	22.86 cm	=	0.23 m
3/8 yard	=	34.29 cm	=	0.34 m
1/2 yard	=	45.72 cm	=	0.46 m
5/8 yard	=	57.15 cm	=	0.57 m
3/4 yard	=	68.58 cm	=	0.69 m
7/8 yard	=	80.00 cm	=	0.80 m
1 yard	=	91.44 cm	=	0.91 m

Resources

Purple Haze on Summer Daze: Spring Fling fabric collection by Terry Atkinson and Liz Lois for P&B Textiles. Machine-quilted by Jane Pitt of Handcrafted Inspirations, Bloomington, Ind. (813) 339-6531. P&B Textiles, 1580 Gilbreth Rd., Burlingame, CA 84010, (650) 692-0422, www.pbtex.com.

Stars Over Paris: Paris Flea Market fabric collection from Moda. United Notions/Moda Fabrics, 13800 Hutton, Dallas, TX 75234, (800) 527-9447, www.modafabrics.com.

Hexagons used to make multiple stencils made by Accu-Cut Systems, 1035 E. Dodge St., Fremont, NE 68025, (800) 288-1670, www.accucut.com.

Susan K. Cleveland's Groovin' Piping Trimming Tool is included in her Piping Hot Binding Kit. Contact her at 54336 237 Ave., West Concord, MN 55985 or at www.PiecesBeWithYou.com or SusanCleveland@att.net.

E-mail: Customer_Service@whitebirches.com

HOUSE of WHITE BIRCHES
PUBLISHERS SINCE 1947

Learn English Paper Piecing by Machine is published by House of White Birches, 306 East Parr Road, Berne, IN 46711, telephone (260) 589-4000. Printed in USA. Copyright © 2005 House of White Birches.

RETAILERS: If you would like to carry this pattern book or any other House of White Birches publications, call the Wholesale Department at Annie's Attic to set up a direct account: (903) 636-4303. Also, request a complete listing of publications available from House of White Birches.

Every effort has been made to ensure that the instructions in this pattern book are complete and accurate. We cannot, however, take responsibility for human error, typographical mistakes or variations in individual work.

ISBN: 1-59217-058-7
1 2 3 4 5 6 7 8 9

STAFF
Editors: Jeanne Stauffer, Sandra L. Hatch
Associate Editor: Dianne Schmidt
Technical Artist: Connie Rand
Copy Supervisor: Michelle Beck
Copy Editors: Nicki Lehman, Beverly Richardson
Graphic Arts Supervisor: Ronda Bechinski

Graphic Artists: Debby Keel, Edith Teegarden
Art Director: Brad Snow
Assistant Art Director: Nick Pierce
Photography: Christena Green, Matthew Owen
Photo Stylist: Tammy Nussbaum, Tammy Smith